FAITH TALES
Family Celebration Edition!

Story Retold by BEVERLY CAPPS BURGESS

Illustrations by ELIZABETH LINDER

A Little Castle Book Harrison House

All Scripture quotations are taken from
the *King James Version* of the Bible.

Faith Tales —
Family Celebration Edition!
ISBN 0-89274-807-9
Copyright © 1991 by Beverly Capps Burgess
P.O. Box 520
Broken Arrow, Oklahoma 74013

Published by **Little Castle Books**
P. O. Box 35035
Tulsa, Oklahoma 74153

Contents

Presented

to

_____

by

_____

_____

Date

THE THREE LITTLE PIGS

Building Your House Upon the Rock

Once upon a time
There were three little pigs.
They were now old enough to be
On their own. All three pigs
Were going to build a home.

*Except the Lord build the house,
they labour in vain that build it....*
Psalm 127:1

The first little pig
Had money and fame.
Unfortunately, he did not know
The power in Jesus' name.

For what is a man profited, if he shall gain
the whole world, and lose his own soul?...
Matthew 16:26

He built his house with money
And trusted in riches.
When the devil came with poverty,
He lost everything,
Even his britches.

For we brought nothing into this world,
and it is certain we can carry nothing out.
1 Timothy 6:7

You see, this is the reason
The devil could do him in,
For he didn't know Jesus
And was living in sin.

Be sober, be vigilant; because your adversary the devil,
as a roaring lion, walketh about, seeking whom he may devour.
1 Peter 5:8

The second little pig thought
He was very smart. He built his
House with a lot of friends
And just knew it could never fall apart!

*Jesus said, Every kingdom divided against itself is brought to desolation;
and every city or house divided against itself shall not stand.*
Matthew 12:25

He was sure his friends would always care;
But when he needed them, they were not there.

And every one that heareth these sayings of mine, and doeth them not,
shall be likened unto a foolish man, which built his house upon the sand:
and the rain descended, and the floods came, and the winds blew,
and beat upon that house; and it fell: and great was the fall of it.
Matthew 7:26,27

Trust not in a neighbor, put not confidence in a friend....
Micah 7:5 AMP

Soon the devil came to his house
With sickness and disease.
The second little pig gave in for he
Didn't know that Jesus had set him free.

If the Son therefore shall make you free,
ye shall be free indeed.
John 8:36

The third little pig
Knew Jesus as his Savior.
When he went to build his house,
He knew he had favor.

So shalt thou find favour and good
understanding in the sight of God and man.
Proverbs 3:4

You see, the third little pig
Built his house upon God's Word.
He knew the word of faith and
Practiced what he had heard.

Therefore whosoever heareth these sayings of mine, and doeth them,
I will liken him unto a wise man, which built his house upon a rock:
and the rain descended, and the floods came, and the winds blew,
and beat upon that house; and it fell not: for it was founded upon a rock.
Matthew 7:24,25

When the devil came
With sickness and disease
And knocked on his door,
He just quoted to him 1 Peter 2:24.

Who his own self bare our sins in his own body on the tree,
that we, being dead to sins, should live unto righteousness:
by whose stripes ye were healed.
1 Peter 2:24

The third little pig trusted in the Lord
And leaned not to his own understanding,
So trusting in riches was not even tempting.

Trust in the Lord with all thine heart;
and lean not unto thine own understanding.
Proverbs 3:5

The third little pig
Knew God was his Source.
He paid tithes and gave,
As the Lord led him, of course.

Give, and it shall be given unto you; good measure, pressed down,
and shaken together, and running over, shall men give into your bosom.
For with the same measure that ye mete withal it shall be measured to you again.
Luke 6:38

He was a great blessing
To all those around.
He told them of the relationship
With Jesus he had found.

The mouth of a righteous man is a well of life....
Proverbs 10:11

God prospered all that the
Third little pig set his hand to do.
If you will give your life to Jesus,
He will do the same for you.

The Lord shall command the blessing upon thee in thy
storehouses, and in all that thou settest thine hand unto; and
he shall bless thee in the land which the Lord thy God giveth thee.
Deuteronomy 28:8

A happy ending...

The third little pig shared Jesus with the other two.
They both were saved and built their lives anew.

And when he had brought them into his house, he set meat
before them, and rejoiced, believing in God with all his house.
Acts 16:34

If you would like to accept Jesus as your Savior, you can pray this prayer now. After you pray, write your name and the date on the lines below.

"Jesus, I thank You for dying for me on the cross. I believe in my heart that God raised You from the dead and You are living today. Please come into my heart and be my Lord forever. Amen."

_____ accepts Jesus as Lord _____, _____.
(Name)   (Month, Day, Year)

JACK AND THE BEANSTALK

Faith As a Seed

Once upon a time, there was a little boy named Jack.
He lived with his poor, old mother in a tiny, little shack.
The only thing they owned was a skinny cow
With a crook in her back.

Mother said to Jack, "The cupboard is now bare, and
even though I've prayed, it seems God doesn't care. I guess
when we get to heaven, it will be much better up there."

Hosea 4:6 — 1 Peter 5:7

24

"Our cow is not worth much, Jack, but sell her anyway.
Maybe you can get sixpence from someone in town today."
Jack felt terrible, but he took the cow and went on his way.

Halfway to town, Jack met a happy old man with a glowing
Smile on his face and a Bible in his hand. He looked at Jack
And said, "Son, I'd like to buy that cow if I can."

Matthew 5:14,15

25

Jack smiled and replied, "Yes, sir! What would you pay?

"Well, let's see... I believe sixpence would be a fair
Price for her today. And I would also give you my Bible
And these beans if I may!"

Jack looked rather surprised and said, "That would be fine!
I can hardly believe that the Bible and beans are all mine!"

The old man said, "Plant them, son, and they will grow in time."

Matthew 5:16 — Mark 4:26-28

"Read the Bible," the old man said, "and you will find
Out how to live in God's blessings without having to sell
Your cow. Faith is like a seed, and it must be planted now."

Jack ran home and told his mother about the wonderful trade.
They laughed and rejoiced about the money they had made.

But Jack kept thinking about what the old man had to say...

John 6:63 — Proverbs 4:20-22

That night while Jack was sleeping soundly in his own
Little bed, he dreamed of planting the beanseed as the old
Man had said. Then suddenly it began growing right up to
Heaven, taking along Jack and his bed!

"Well," thought Jack, "maybe God can explain what that man told
Me about living in God's blessings and faith being like a seed."

Then a voice spoke boldly, "Yes, Jack, I can help you indeed!"

Acts 2:17 — 1 Corinthians 2:9,10

28

God spoke to Jack again and said, "All that I have belongs
To you. You need to learn what My Word says for you to do.
Then you will prosper and be in health as I *want* you to!

"Think on My words day and night, then you will have
Good success. You will find out I am not the one who
Puts you to the test. All I want is for My children
To always have the best."

Luke 15:30 — Joshua 1:8

"It's the devil," God said, "who steals, kills, and destroys.
But I have given you power over all the enemy's ploys.
To those who know the power in Jesus' name,
The devil's roaring is only noise!

"The devil has been devouring all My blessings that were
Meant for you. But you can plant your faith by speaking
My words like I created you to do, and your seed of faith
Will produce a crop of blessings made just for you.

John 10:10 — 1 Peter 5:8

"When My children are overflowing with the good
Things that belong to Me, they can reach out to others
And set the captives free, so that people everywhere
Will know I am a God of love and mercy."

Jack said, "Oh, thank You, Lord, for now I understand.
I am going to read my Bible as often as I can,
And I will be a doer of Your Word over and over again!"

Luke 4:18 — James 1:22

31

God warned Jack, "I believe you will, My son, but you
Must beware... There is a roaming giant of unbelief down
There. Don't let him trick you into his snare."

"No, Sir, I won't," said Jack as he slid down through the sky
On a beanstalk that must have been two hundred miles high!

"I will remember what You said!"
Yelled Jack as he waved goodbye.

Matthew 13:58 — John 14:26

Jack awakened to his mother's voice,
"Get up, son, it's 8:15."

He slumped in his bed thinking,
"Oh, it was only a dream.
Surely I can't change things by the way
I talk and believe."

Mark 11:23

It was that huge old giant,
Sneaking up on poor little Jack.

Then Jack remembered what God had said...
How the giant would attack.

So Jack yelled bravely,
"I believe God's Word! So, giant, you get back!"

Ephesians 6:10,11

34

That huge old giant ran away as fast as he could.

Then Jack and his mother studied the Word as they should.

They found every promise in God's Word
That Jack had dreamed about.

And they lived happily ever after
Serving God without a doubt.

And they never again lacked for any good thing!

John 8:31,32

My God shall supply all your needs
according to His riches in glory by Christ Jesus.
Philippians 4:19

CHICKEN LITTLE
CONQUERS FEAR

One Sunday morning bright and early Chicken Little
Went outside to play. He was dressed in his nicest suit.
He was going to church on a beautiful day!

When suddenly an acorn from the tree above Fell and hit
Chicken Little right on the head. Chicken Little screamed,
"Oh, no! The sky is falling, And soon we will all be dead!"

This is the day which the Lord hath made; we will rejoice and be glad in it.
Psalm 118:24

Peace I leave with you, my peace I give unto you: not as the world giveth,
give I unto you. Let not your heart be troubled, neither let it be afraid.
John 14:27

"**I** shall run and tell the King. That is all that I can do. . . .
I can't imagine that such a horrible thing could happen.
And on a Sunday too!"

He ran and he ran and soon he saw
Turkey Lurkey walking with a Bible in his hand.
"Turkey Lurkey, the sky is falling,
And we must warn all those in the land!"

There shall no evil befall thee, neither shall any plague come nigh thy dwelling.
Psalm 91:10

Be not afraid of sudden fear, neither of the desolation of the wicked, when it cometh.
For the Lord shall be thy confidence, and shall keep thy foot from being taken.
Proverbs 3:25,26

"**H**ow do you know the sky is falling?"
Turkey Lurkey asked.

"Because I saw it, I felt it, and I heard it,"
Chicken Little replied.

"I *was* going to church,

But this is much more important," Turkey Lurkey sighed.

(For we walk by faith, not by sight:).
2 Corinthians 5:7

It was only a short while till they saw Goosey Poosey.
He had his Sunday hat on, and his shoes shined.
"Should we tell him?" asked Chicken Little.
Turkey Lurkey answered, "If we didn't, it would be unkind."

"Goosey Poosey, you must come with us.
The sky is falling — it is a terrible thing.
We must all go quickly to the palace. There we can warn the King."

Finally, brethren, whatsoever things are true, whatsoever things are honest, whatsoever things are just,
whatsoever things are pure, whatsoever things are lovely, whatsoever things are of good report;
if there be any virtue, and if there be any praise, think on these things.
Philippians 4:8

The tongue of the wise useth knowledge aright: but the mouth of fools poureth out foolishness.
Proverbs 15:2

"**O**h, my,'' said Goosey Poosey.
"How do you know the sky is falling?''

"Because I saw it, I felt it, and I heard it,'' said Chicken Little.

"And I believe every word he says,''
Goosey Poosey confirmed.

Chicken Little and Turkey Lurkey left with
Goosey Poosey in the middle.

The simple believeth every word: but the prudent man looketh well to his going.
Proverbs 14:15

Just before they reached the town, they saw Cockey Lockey.
"Where are you going in such a hurry?" he wanted to know.
"Haven't you heard the sky is falling?
We are going to tell the King. Will you go?"

"After all," said Chicken Little, "I know it's true. I saw it,
I felt it, and I heard it too." "They surely won't miss ME at church,"
Thought Cockey Lockey. "I think I will come along too!"

The heart of him that hath understanding seeketh knowledge:
but the mouth of fools feedeth on foolishness.
Proverbs 15:14

While we look not at the things which are seen, but at the things which are not seen:
for the things which are seen are temporal; but the things which are not seen are eternal.
2 Corinthians 4:18

After many hours of traveling, they reached the palace.

"We must see the King," they told the guards at the gate.

"Sorry," they said, "he is at church."

"Oh, no!" Chicken Little cried. "It's going to be too late!"

In righteousness shalt thou be established: thou shalt be far from oppression;
for thou shalt not fear: and from terror; for it shall not come near thee."
Isaiah 54:14

Just then the King's carriage arrived.
The King stepped out with a smile on his face.
"What can I do for you, young man?" he asked,
As he walked toward them with grace.

"Oh, King, it is a terrible thing.
The sky is falling and we had to tell you.
We knew that you would be able to tell us what to do."

Great peace have they which love thy law: and nothing shall offend them.
Psalm 119:165

If any of you lack wisdom, let him ask of God, that giveth to all men liberally,
and upbraideth not; and it shall be given him.
James 1:5

The King said to Chicken Little,
"Son, this doesn't make much sense at all.
Why are you so upset? And why do you think that the sky will fall?"

"Because I saw it, I felt it, and I heard it.
And that's reason enough," Chicken Little spoke out.
"Well," said the King, "I don't mean to sound skeptical,
But I do have my doubts."

*There is no fear in love; but perfect love casteth out fear: because
fear hath torment. He that feareth is not made perfect in love.*
1 John 4:18

*A thousand shall fall at thy side, and ten thousand at
thy right hand; but it shall not come nigh thee.*
Psalm 91:7

"You see, God doesn't give us the spirit of fear.
He doesn't lead us by what we feel, see, or hear,
But by His Holy Spirit, through Jesus Christ, who is always near.

"He has given His angels charge over us.
They keep us in all our ways.
It seems to me, you have been letting fear
Rule in your heart all day!"

For God hath not given us the spirit of fear;
but of power, and of love and of a sound mind.
2 Timothy 1:7

For he shall give his angels charge over thee, to keep thee in all thy ways.
Psalm 91:11

45

"You see, if your trust is truly in the Lord,
You won't be moved when things LOOK bad.
Because you will know God's Word is true.
And you will never have a reason to be sad.

"It seems to me your problem is, you haven't fed your heart.
You feed it God's Word by going to church and reading
the Bible. And now is a good time for you to start."

In God have I put my trust: I will not be afraid what man can do unto me.
Psalm 56:11

And Jesus answered him, saying, It is written, That man
shall not live by bread alone, but by every word of God.
Luke 4:4

The King spoke to the others...
"As for the rest of you, do you see how fear can spread?
If it weren't for believing lies, you'd be at church,
Instead of thinking you'll soon be dead.

"I hope you have all learned your lesson well.
Fear is not of God, so be careful what you hear.
Protecting your heart sometimes will mean also covering your ears."

The Lord is my light and my salvation; whom shall I fear?
the Lord is the strength of my life; of whom shall I be afraid?

Though an host should encamp against me, my heart shall not fear:
though war should rise against me, in this will I be confident.
Psalm 27:1,3

Keep thy heart with all diligence; for out of it are the issues of life.
Proverbs 4:23

Chicken Little, Turkey Lurkey, Goosey Poosey
And Cockey Lockey
Were the first ones at church that night.
From that day on they read and studied the Word of God
With all their might.

If you will study God's Word and get it into your heart,
You can keep fear far away from you.
And you are never too young to start!

Poverty and shame shall be to him that refuseth instruction:
but he that regardeth reproof shall be honoured.
Proverbs 13:18

Study to shew thyself approved unto God, a workman that needeth
not to be ashamed, rightly dividing the word of truth.
2 Timothy 2:15

LITTLE RED RIDINGHOOD

Once upon a time
There was a little girl named Red Ridinghood.
She had a little old grandmother
Who lived deep in the woods.

When I call to remembrance the unfeigned faith that is in thee,
which dwelt first in thy grandmother Lois, and thy mother Eunice;
and I am persuaded that in thee also.
2 Timothy 1:5

The grandmother was a Christian
But didn't know much of God's Word.
She needed to be healed is
What Red Ridinghood had heard.

My people are destroyed for lack of knowledge.
Hosea 4:6

The devil kept trying to hurt Grandma
With sickness, poverty, and disease.
Red Ridinghood was bringing her
God's Word to set her free.

And ye shall know the truth, and the truth shall make you free.
John 8:32

Red Ridinghood left
To visit her grandmother,
Saying, "I lay hands on the sick,
And they do recover."

And these signs shall follow them that believe:
In my name shall they. . .lay hands on the sick, and they shall recover.
Mark 16:17,18

_She knew the mean old devil
Would try to stop her if he could,
So she prayed in the spirit
As she knew she should.

Be sober, be vigilant; because your adversary the devil,
as a roaring lion, walketh about, seeking whom he may devour.
1 Peter 5:8

Red Ridinghood had no spirit of fear.
She knew that because of God's love,
He is always near.

For God hath not given us the spirit of fear;
but of power, and of love, and of a sound mind.
2 Timothy 1:7

The mean old devil didn't have a chance,
When he heard Red Ridinghood pray,
He left so fast
He lost his pants.

Resist the devil, and he will flee from you.
James 4:7

Grandma was so happy to see
Little Red Ridinghood.
She asked, "Why am I so sick
When God is so good?"

I am the good shepherd, and know my sheep,
and am known of mine.
John 10:14

Little Red Ridinghood explained how it
Was the devil making her sick and not God,
And that her feet with the preparation of
The Gospel must be shod.

The thief cometh not, but for to steal, and to kill, and to destroy:
I am come that they might have life, and that they might have it more abundantly.
John 10:10

And your feet shod with the preparation of the gospel of peace.
Ephesians 6:15

Grandma's faith grew as
Little Red Ridinghood talked.
She laid hands on Grandma and said,
"In the name of Jesus, rise up and walk."

So then faith cometh by hearing,
and hearing by the word of God.
Romans 10:17

Grandma instantly received her healing.
She praised and thanked God
While walking and leaping.

*And he leaping up stood, and walked, and entered with them
into the temple, walking, and leaping, and praising God.*
Acts 3:8

Little Red Ridinghood explained how
Grandma should read and study her Bible:
"God's words are spirit and life —
The key to your survival."

It is the spirit that quickeneth; the flesh profiteth nothing:
the words that I speak unto you, they are spirit, and they are life.
John 6:63

Grandma did just what the Word said.
She learned to walk in divine health
Instead of being sick in bed.

But be ye doers of the word,
and not hearers only, deceiving your own selves.
James 1:22

This made Little Red Ridinghood
Very happy, too,
For she loved her grandma very much,
Just like you!

Beloved, let us love one another: for love is of God;
and every one that loveth is born of God, and knoweth God.
1 John 4:7

THE THREE BEARS
IN THE MINISTRY

Once upon a time,
There were three bears:
Mama Bear, Papa Bear, and Baby Bear.
They were very happy because upon
Jesus they had cast every care.

Casting all your care upon him; for he careth for you.
1 Peter 5:7

Papa Bear was called to be an evangelist.
All day they had been out preaching.
They came home praising God and singing.

Make a joyful noise unto God, all ye lands:
Sing forth the honour of his name: make his praise glorious.
Psalm 66:1,2

As the bears walked in,
They knew someone was in the house.
But they were not afraid.
Papa Bear told Baby Bear,
''Be quiet as a mouse.''

Fear thou not; for I am with thee: be not dismayed; for I am thy God:
I will strengthen thee; yea, I will help thee;
yea, I will uphold thee with the right hand of my righteousness.
Isaiah 41:10

Mama Bear found Goldilocks asleep in Baby Bear's bed.
Papa Bear prayed in the Spirit to know what to do.
Then he awoke Goldilocks and gently said...

*Likewise the Spirit also helpeth our infirmities: for we know not
what we should pray for as we ought: but the Spirit itself maketh
intercession for us with groanings which cannot be uttered.*

*And he that searcheth the hearts knoweth what is the mind of the Spirit,
because he maketh intercession for the saints according to the will of God.*
Romans 8:26,27

"**H**oney, the Lord told me that you've run away.
God loves you very much.
He wants you to be born again today!"

. . . Except a man be born again, he cannot see the kingdom of God.
John 3:3

Goldilocks began to cry,
"I ran away because I was so mad.
I really do love my Mom and my Dad.
Tell me how to make Jesus my Lord.
I feel so very bad."

Children, obey your parents in the Lord:
for this is right.
Ephesians 6:1

Mama Bear opened her Bible
And read Romans 10:9,10.
Baby Bear explained to Goldilocks
How Jesus died for her sin.

If thou shalt confess with thy mouth the Lord Jesus,
and shalt believe in thine heart that God hath raised
him from the dead, thou shalt be saved.
Romans 10:9,10

Goldilocks prayed and
Asked forgiveness for her unbelief.
She confessed Jesus as Lord and
Believed God that His promises He will keep.

And when he is come, he will reprove the world of sin,
and of righteousness, and of judgment.
John 16:8

Everyone was joyful. Papa Bear said,
''Now that you are born again, you will need power.
The Holy Spirit is given and is for this hour.''

But ye shall receive power, after that the Holy Ghost
is come upon you: and ye shall be witnesses unto me
both in Jerusalem, and in all Judea, and in Samaria,
and unto the uttermost part of the earth.
Acts 1:8

Papa Bear turned to Acts 2:4.
He read that scripture and several more.
Mama Bear and Baby Bear prayed in the
Spirit quietly, while sitting on the floor.

*And they were all filled with the Holy Ghost, and began to
speak with other tongues, as the Spirit gave them utterance.*
Acts 2:4

Papa Bear laid hands on Goldilocks
And said, ''Receive ye the Holy Spirit.''
Goldilocks raised her hands and began to speak
In other tongues where everyone could hear it.

Thus will I bless thee while I live:
I will lift up my hands in thy name.
Psalm 63:4

When through praying,
Goldilocks thought twice.
She exclaimed, "I have to go tell my parents
I'm a new creature in Christ."

Therefore if any man be in Christ, he is a new creature:
old things are passed away; behold, all things are become new.
2 Corinthians 5:17

The three Bears took
Goldilocks home in their car.
She was ready to minister to her parents
And was so glad it wasn't very far.

Whosoever therefore shall confess me before men,
him will I confess also before my Father which is in heaven.
Matthew 10:32

When they arrived, Goldilocks gave
Her testimony of what the Lord had done.
Right then, her family was born again
And filled with the Holy Spirit
— each and every one!

And all things are of God, who hath reconciled us to himself by
Jesus Christ, and hath given to us the ministry of reconciliation.
2 Corinthians 5:18

LITTLE RED HEN

Once upon a time, there was a Little Red Hen,
Who loved God with all of her heart.

She had asked Jesus to be her Lord,
And wanted to please Him from the start!

*That if thou shalt confess with thy mouth the Lord Jesus, and shalt believe
in thine heart that God hath raised him from the dead, thou shalt be saved.*

*For with the heart man believeth unto righteousness;
and with the mouth confession is made unto salvation.*
Romans 10:9,10

She had three neighbors at the
Farm who were Christians, too.

They all went to church and heard the Word,
But Little Red Hen did the things God said to do!

But whoso keepeth his word, in him verily is the love of God perfected:
hereby know we that we are in him.
1 John 2:5

Little Red Hen read the Bible each day.
"Who would like to read with me?" she asked her friends.

"Not I," said Mr. Duck. "I'm taking a trip to town."

"Not I," said Mrs. Cat. "I am going to lie down."

"Not I," grumbled Mr. Pig. **"I don't have time!"**

So she read the Word anyway!

My son, attend to my words; incline thine ear unto my sayings.
Let them not depart from thine eyes; keep them in the midst of thine heart.
Proverbs 4:20

My son, keep my words, and lay up my commandments with thee.
Proverbs 7:1

The Little Red Hen loved to pray.
"Would you like to pray also?" she asked her friends.

"Not I," said Mr. Duck. "I don't have a need."

"Not I," said Mrs. Cat. "I have too many kittens to feed."

"Not I," grumbled Mr. Pig. **"I don't have time."**

But Little Red Hen kept right on praying!

Pray without ceasing.
1 Thessalonians 5:17

Little Red Hen was very sad
Because she knew her friends were missing God's best.

They were too lazy to do the Word of God
And put it to the test!

When any one heareth the word of the kingdom, and understandeth it not,
then cometh the wicked one, and catcheth away that which was sown in
his heart. This is he which received seed by the way side.
Matthew 13:19

I know, she thought, *I will have a Bible study and help them learn the Word.*

"Will you come?" she asked them hopefully.

"Not I," said Mr. Duck. "I just want to have fun."

"Not I," said Mrs. Cat. "I am going to visit my son."

"Not I," grumbled Mr. Pig. **"I don't have time."**

Go ye therefore, and teach all nations, baptizing them in the name of the Father, and of the Son, and of the Holy Ghost:
Matthew 28:19,20

All this time the Little Red Hen
Took very good care of her family.

She spent plenty of time with them
And kept her house clean, you see.

God helped the Little Red Hen with everything she did.

She even trusted God to help her raise her kids!

She looketh well to the ways of her household, and eateth not the bread of idleness.
Her children arise up, and call her blessed; her husband also, and he praiseth her.
Proverbs 31:27,28

Little Red Hen knew that the winter snow was coming.

But her trust was in the Word, and she used her head!

She wanted to prepare her home with straw to keep it
Warm, and gather lots of food to keep her family fed.

She stretcheth out her hand to the poor; yea, she reacheth forth her hands to the needy.
She is not afraid of the snow for her household:
for all her household are clothed with scarlet.
Proverbs 31:20,21

Then Little Red Hen thought of
Something she could do...

I will help my neighbors prepare their homes,
And they can help me prepare mine, too!

Therefore all things whatsoever ye would that men should do to you,
do ye even so to them: for this is the law and the prophets.
Matthew 7:12

"**W**ould you like for me to help you prepare
Your house for winter?" she asked. "If we worked
Together, it would be much easier."

"Not I," said Mr. Duck. "I'm too old."

"Not I," said Mrs. Cat. "I never get cold"

"Not I," grumbled Mr. Pig. **"I don't have time."**

So Little Red Hen went home and did it all by herself!

Give her of the fruit of her hands; and let her own works praise her in the gates.
Proverbs 31:31

When winter came, the snow was piled up very high. Little
Red Hen was warm and cozy, and her house was very dry.

But deep inside she felt so sad because she knew
Her friends were cold. And she thought of poor
Mr. Duck who was getting very old!

Then she had a wonderful idea...

If a man say, I love God, and hateth his brother, he is a liar: for he that loveth not
his brother whom he hath seen, how can he love God whom he hath not seen?
1 John 4:20

Little Red Hen ran out into the deep snow
And called her neighbors together.

"Will you come into my warm house and stay
For the winter?" She asked. "I have more than
Enough room for you all."

"I will!" said Mr. Duck.
"I will!" said Mrs. Cat.
"I will, too!" said Mr. Pig in his nicest tone of voice.

But whoso hath this world's good, and seeth his brother have need, and
shutteth up his bowels of compassion from him, how dwelleth the love of God in him?
1 John 3:17

All winter long, Little Red Hen
Taught her neighbors God's Word.

She prayed with them and shared the
Faith of God that she had heard.

*Hereby perceive we the love of God, because he laid down his life for us:
and we ought to lay down our lives for the brethren.*
1 John 3:16

After that winter, Mr. Duck and Mrs. Cat and Mr. Pig were not lazy Christians anymore.

They did *all* that God's Word said to do.

God blessed them; and if you are a doer of the Word, He will bless you, too!

If ye be willing and obedient, ye shall eat the good of the land.
Isaiah 1:19

Other Little Castle Books
by
Beverly Capps Burgess

*Seedtime
Stories*

*Prayers
for Pre-Schoolers*

*God Is Never
Too Busy To Listen*

God Is My Best Friend

God, Are You Really Real?

Is Easter Just for Bunnies?

How Can I Please You, God?

Individual Faith Tales

Additional Bestselling Books
From the Little Castle Library

*Prayers That Avail Much
For Children*
Angela Brown

*Prayers That Avail Much
For Children*
Book 2

*The Flight of Orville Wright
CaterPillar*
Donna Perugini

Don't Hug a Grudge
Donna Perugini

Do Angels Go Camping?
Donna Perugini

Confessions for Kids
Harrison House

*The Bird With the Word
Talks About the
Fruits of the Spirit*
9-book series
by Claudia Tarpley Rees
*Love/Joy/Peace/Patience
Kindness/Goodness/Faith
Self-Control*

Available from your local bookstore, or from:

HARRISON HOUSE
P. O. Box 35035
Tulsa, OK 74153

Dear Friend,

As a believer and a responsible parent, it is so important for you to fill your child with God's Word. Our goal in this book is to engraft the Word of God into the child by applying the Word in a story that has been passed down for years. Your child will be able to see by example how to minister effectively and how to apply the Word in his or her own life.

The Scripture references on each page help you to relate the story and illustrations to the biblical principles you desire to develop in your child. Be faithful in reading and training your child in God's Word!

If your child has questions about some of the words or Scripture verses in these stories, take time to define the words and explain the scriptures. Children are capable of understanding much more than we give them credit for. Avoid limiting your child's knowledge by simplifying things too much! Remember that training your child requires you to give of your time and your love.

*In Him,
Bill and Beverly Burgess*